WHY
EASTER
MATTERS

ANDY STANLEY

NORTH POINT
RESOURCES

ZONDERVAN™

ZONDERVAN
Why Easter Matters Study Guide
Copyright © 2019 by North Point Ministries, Inc.

Requests for information should be addressed to:
Zondervan, *3900 Sparks Dr. SE, Grand Rapids, Michigan 49546*

ISBN 978-0-310-12109-1 (softcover)
ISBN 978-0-310-12110-7 (ebook)

First Printing September 2019 / Printed in the United States of America

HB 03.04.2024

[CONTENTS]

USING THE
STUDY GUIDE

BEFORE THE FIRST GROUP MEETING

Read through the Introduction for an overview of the study.

Flip through pages 11–20 to understand the layout of a session.

DURING EACH GROUP MEETING

1. Turn to the Video Notes page and watch the video segment.

2. Use the Discussion Questions to have a conversation about the video content.

AFTER EACH GROUP MEETING

On your own, read the Think About It section.

Review the Before the Next Session section at the end of each session and complete the tasks.

USING THE
STUDY GUIDE

[INTRODUCTION]

One of the things that baffles non-Christians about Christians is how often Christians resist the God they say they trust. Let's be honest: If you're a Christian, you'd probably say that at some point in your life—maybe today—you've had an internal battle with God. Have you ever found yourself resisting the God you say you trust? We all have.

Maybe you knew you should forgive someone who'd wronged you, but it was hard—*really* hard. Maybe you were in an unhealthy relationship and you knew you should get out, but something about the relationship was fascinating, even a little addictive. Maybe you knew you shouldn't go to a certain place, but you did anyway because you were afraid of missing out. Maybe you knew you shouldn't spend money irresponsibly and you should be more generous, but the temptation to indulge yourself was irresistible.

Your conscience tells you what's right. The Scriptures tell you what's right. You're trying to be a Jesus follower, but you just want to do what you want to do. You find yourself resisting the God you trust.

Non-Christians have a word for this: *hypocrisy*. They're not wrong. When we don't walk our talk, we're hypocrites. It's best to just own that. But be merciful with yourself and others. It's difficult to surrender your life to a God you've never seen. It's difficult to surrender your life to a God who speaks to your heart and mind through your conscience and ancient literature.

This is the ongoing struggle. Even non-Christians understand this battle. Every person, believer or nonbeliever, knows what it's like to wrestle with their conscience. It's just a part of the human condition: we apply standards to our lives that we have trouble living up to.

During the four sessions of this study, we're going to take a look at three people whose lives intersected Jesus' life in the weeks leading up to his crucifixion. Each of them had an agenda that put them at odds with God and with Jesus. And as we're going to see, there's a little bit of them in all of us.

But here's what's interesting: *Their stories of resistance illustrate the futility of resisting God.*

If you've been a Christian for long, you know that your story of resistance is also an illustration of the futility of resisting God. In fact, every person's life—believer or nonbeliever—is a story of resisting God. And every person's life is an illustration of the futility of resisting God.

That's why Easter matters.

SESSION ONE

[THE HIGH COST OF FOLLOWING CHRIST]

The first character we're going to talk about in this study is Joseph Caiaphas. If you grew up in church, you probably know him as Caiaphas. He was the high priest during the time of Jesus—the most powerful, influential person in Jerusalem, Judea, and what we would consider ancient Israel. He was the connecting point between the nation of Israel and the Roman Empire. He was the person that communicated with Pilate and other leaders.

Even more important, Caiaphas was part of a family that controlled the temple for 40 years. His father-in-law and five of his brothers-in-law were high priests. They had enormous power and influence.

They were extraordinarily wealthy. There were amazing financial perks that came with being at the epicenter of the Jewish religion in the first century. Jews all over the world paid a temple tax to support the operation and upkeep of the temple in Jerusalem as well as to pay the priests and high priests.

Life was pretty good for Caiaphas until a carpenter-turned-rabbi stepped onto the pages of history . . .

OVERVIEW

Everywhere Jesus went, hundreds or even thousands of people followed. The crowds were enormous. This was a threat to Rome. And it was a threat to the Jewish religious establishment because crowds in first-century Judea tended to lead to division and insurrection. Crowds made Rome nervous. That put pressure on Caiaphas, because one of the things Rome expected of him was to maintain the peace by keeping his own people under control.

The other problem Jesus posed to Caiaphas was that when he spoke, he spoke with authority. People were amazed by Jesus' authority. He behaved and spoke with extraordinary confidence. And he was critical of the religious leaders.

Because of the corruption inside the temple system, Jesus took the temple leaders to task. Matthew 23 offers a startling example of Jesus' passionate criticism of a system that had grown to exploit the very people it was meant to serve. He goes on and on about the hypocrisy of the religious leaders, even saying:

"You snakes! You brood of vipers! How will you escape being condemned to hell?" Matthew 23:33

That's harsh. It's no wonder Caiaphas had a problem with Jesus given Jesus' authority, the crowds he drew, and his criticism of everybody Caiaphas worked with and respected. Jesus threatened the peace and the peacekeepers. He was challenging the foundations of Caiaphas' power and wealth. He was challenging the foundations of his life.

But the final straw between Jesus and Caiaphas wasn't something Jesus said. It was something he did—an act of compassion. Jesus raised Lazarus from the dead. Lazarus had been dead and buried. The people in his hometown of Bethany had been to the funeral. So, when Lazarus came back to life and was walking around again, the crowds around Jesus swelled to unprecedented sizes. John's Gospel says:

Meanwhile a large crowd of Jews found out that Jesus was there and came, not only because of him but also to see Lazarus, whom he had raised from the dead.
John 12:9

Caiaphas realized his strategy of trying to publicly discredit Jesus wasn't working. He and the other religious leaders had worked hard to ask Jesus trick questions that would force him to either betray God or threaten the Roman Empire. But Jesus always outsmarted them—not because he was evasive with his answers or was good at playing political games. Jesus rejected the assumptions at the core of the religious leaders' questions.

When they asked him if people should pay taxes to Rome or give that money to God, Jesus responded: "Give back to Caesar what is Caesar's and to God what is God's." Jesus was saying that money played a much less significant role in God's kingdom than the religious leaders believed—their priorities were all wrong. But after Lazarus, Caiaphas realized that these little traps weren't going to work.

> Then the chief priests and the Pharisees called a meeting of the Sanhedrin.
>
> "What are we accomplishing?" they asked. "Here is this man performing many signs. If we let him go on like this, everyone will believe in him, and then the Romans will come and take away both our temple and our nation."
>
> Then one of them, named Caiaphas, who was high priest that year, spoke up, "You know nothing at all! You do not realize that it is better for you that one man

die for the people than that the whole nation perish."
John 11:47–50

The big worry of the religious leaders was that everyone would believe in Jesus. In their heart of hearts, they knew that to resist Jesus was to resist God. But following Jesus would have required them to let go of something that was important to them—something they'd built their entire lives around. The religious system rewarded and protected them. It defined them. And Jesus was bringing change. *If we don't do something*, they thought, *we are going to lose everything that is important to us.*

So from that day on they plotted to take his life.
John 11:53

When you decide to follow Jesus, it will cost you something. In fact, as a Christian, every single time you decide to put Jesus front and center in your life, it will cost you something. This may be the reason you resisted church for so long.

Eventually, Caiaphas pegged Jesus with the charge of sedition against the Roman Empire, and he had Jesus crucified. The threat was eliminated. Caiaphas' position in the nation was secure. And then just as the sun rose on the first day of the week after Passover, there was commotion in the streets of Jerusalem. The body of Jesus was missing. A few days after that came reports of Jesus sightings all around the area. A few weeks after that, Jesus' closest followers came out of hiding and into the streets of Jerusalem saying, "You crucified Jesus. God raised him from the dead. We've seen him. Say you're sorry."

Suddenly there were crowds of people rallying around the name, reputation, and resurrection of Jesus. And it began to dawn on Caiaphas that Jesus had accomplished more by dying than he had during his lifetime.

Years later, Caiaphas lost his place of leadership. The Jewish people lost their temple when it was torn down by the future Roman emperor Titus in AD 70. Those who attempted to stand against the will of God became footnotes in the story of Jesus. Thus Caiaphas, the influential high priest, became a footnote in the story of Jesus of Nazareth.

What does that have to do with us? Everything. Because there is a little Caiaphas in each of us. There's something inside us that wants to preserve things at all costs. We want God to either help us or get out of our way. But Easter is a warning against that impulse. God does not compromise, and those who try to stand against him will become footnotes.

VIDEO NOTES

_____

_____

_____

_____

_____

_____

_____

_____

_____

_____

_____

_____

_____

_____

_____

_____

_____

_____

_____

_____

_____

DISCUSSION QUESTIONS

1. What do you hope to experience this Easter season? Do you usually observe Easter as a spiritual season, celebrate it as a holiday, or both?

2. During the message, Andy said, "When you decide to follow Jesus, it will cost you something." If you are a Jesus follower, what is something following has cost you?

3. What's intimidating about the idea that God's will can't be thwarted? What's comforting?

4. Read John 11:38–44 aloud as a group. What do verses 41 and 42 indicate about Jesus' intent in raising Lazarus from the dead?

5. Read John 11:45–50 aloud as a group. How do verses 49 and 50 demonstrate the human capacity for justifying wrong-doing? Talk about a time when you convinced yourself that something morally or ethically wrong was the right thing to do. What happened?

6. What are you currently trying to preserve that you need to surrender to God? What is one thing you can do this week to begin to let go? How can this group support you?

THINK ABOUT IT

Whatever is in the center of your life is the thing that has replaced God. It may be a position at work, a grade-point average, an unhealthy relationship, money, power, or sex. Whatever that little voice inside is desperate to preserve is standing between you and your heavenly Father. And the thought of losing that thing probably terrifies you.

But whatever you've replaced God with is less than God. It is already diminishing in value and significance. Think about it. Your greatest regrets are connected to attempts to preserve something or someone that isn't even a part of your life anymore.

Don't let something that doesn't even matter in the long-run act as a "little-g" god in your life. The little gods always disappoint. God doesn't. God has a plan for your life. To put anything other than him at the center of your life is self-destructive.

What are you trying to preserve that you need to surrender to God? What's the little god in your life that is demanding more and more and providing less and less? Saying yes to God will cost you something. Saying no will cost you more, including what you replace God with.

BEFORE THE NEXT SESSION

To prepare for your next session, read the Overview for Session Two.

You can also look through the Discussion Questions if you want to.

During the week, spend some time each day reading John 13.

SESSION TWO

[THE RISK OF SURRENDERING TO GOD]

Have you ever tried to bargain with God?

You're not alone. Regardless of our faith or non-faith, we've all said something along the lines of, "God, what do I need to do to get you to do what I need you to do?" We bargain with our prayers. We bargain with our church attendance. We bargain with our giving.

This session's character tried to get Jesus to do his bidding. And when Jesus wouldn't do what he wanted Jesus to do, this character quit following. He walked away.

The reason we're talking about this character is because there's a little bit of him in all of us. We've all tried to bargain with God.

This session, we're going to talk about Judas Iscariot. For Judas, Jesus was always a means to an end. But before we get critical of Judas as the great villain of the Gospel narrative, let's try to understand his perspective and recognize that it is uncomfortably similar to our own.

OVERVIEW

All of Jesus' disciples struggled with viewing him as a means to an end. To one extent or another, they followed him because they thought there was something in it for them. There's a story in the middle of Matthew's Gospel that illustrates this point:

> Just then a man came up to Jesus and asked, "Teacher, what good thing must I do to get eternal life?"
>
> "Why do you ask me about what is good?" Jesus replied. "There is only One who is good. If you want to enter life, keep the commandments."
>
> "Which ones?" he inquired.
>
> Jesus replied, "'You shall not murder, you shall not commit adultery, you shall not steal, you shall not give false testimony, honor your father and mother,' and 'love your neighbor as yourself.'"

"All these I have kept," the young man said. "What do I still lack?"

Jesus answered, "If you want to be perfect, go, sell your possessions and give to the poor, and you will have treasure in heaven. Then come, follow me."

When the young man heard this, he went away sad, because he had great wealth.

Then Jesus said to his disciples, "Truly I tell you, it is hard for someone who is rich to enter the kingdom of heaven. Again I tell you, it is easier for a camel to go through the eye of a needle than for someone who is rich to enter the kingdom of God." Matthew 19:16–24

What's interesting is Peter's reaction to this idea that it's difficult for rich people to enter the kingdom of God:

Peter answered him, "We have left everything to follow you! What then will there be for us?" Matthew 19:27

What will there be for us? Peter had the nerve to actually ask it, but every Christian has thought that. This was the question Judas asked constantly.

From Judas' perspective, Jesus was a little too passive at times. He wouldn't save enough money. You need money to have a movement, but every time their treasury began to grow, Jesus would give money away. Jesus didn't seem to have enough energy or focus. Judas began to lose patience. Finally, something happened that was the final straw for Judas. It was an extraordinary act of generosity and it sent Judas over the edge.

> Six days before the Passover, Jesus came to Bethany, where Lazarus lived, whom Jesus had raised from the dead. Here a dinner was given in Jesus' honor. Martha served, while Lazarus was among those reclining at the table with him. Then Mary took about a pint of pure nard, an expensive perfume; she poured it on Jesus' feet and wiped his feet with her hair. And the house was filled with the fragrance of the perfume.

> But one of his disciples, Judas Iscariot, who was later to betray him, objected, "Why wasn't this perfume sold and the money given to the poor? It was worth a year's wages." He did not say this because he cared about the poor but because he was a thief; as keeper of the money bag, he used to help himself to what was put into it.

"Leave her alone," Jesus replied. "It was intended that she should save this perfume for the day of my burial. You will always have the poor among you, but you will not always have me." John 12:1–8

Keep in mind that this is from John's Gospel and John was there. He was not only one of the 12 disciples; he was in Jesus' inner circle of followers. And he provided some interesting details. He noted, first of all, that Judas Iscariot was the disciple that took offense at Mary pouring the expensive nard over Jesus' head. John is also blunt about Judas' motive for complaining. He didn't care about the poor. In fact, he used to steal from the group's moneybag.

Yet it was a subtle but odd statement by Jesus that really set Judas off: "It was intended that she should save this perfume for the day of my burial." Burial? Judas hadn't signed on as one of Jesus' disciples in order to see him buried. This Jesus was supposed to be the Messiah.

In the minds of most Jews, the Messiah would rise up as a military leader, drive out the occupying Roman army, and establish Israel as a world power—as the world power. If Jesus was the Messiah, then proximity to him meant great power, wealth, and influence. Being one of the 12 disciples would have its perks. As Judas saw it, burial wasn't part of the plan. Matthew's Gospel tells us what he did next:

> Then one of the Twelve—the one called Judas Iscariot— went to the chief priests and asked, "What are you willing to give me if I deliver him over to you?" So they counted out for him thirty pieces of silver. From then on Judas watched for an opportunity to hand him over.
>
> Matthew 26:14–16

Think about this: Judas was eye to eye with Jesus. He rode on a boat with Jesus. He saw the miracles. They shared meals. Judas was in Jesus' physical presence and he got so fed up because he couldn't get Jesus to do what he thought Jesus should do. Judas traded his relationship with Jesus for 30 pieces of silver.

Think about the things you've been tempted to trade your relationship with Jesus for. They're probably not any more valuable or lasting than 30 pieces of silver. But in the moment, it feels like the right thing to do because it doesn't feel like you're getting anything out of your relationship with Jesus. So, from then on after he made this deal, Judas watched for an opportunity to hand Jesus over. Now, this was when the music changed.

Shortly after Judas made his deal with the high priest, it was time for Passover. On a Thursday afternoon, Jesus sent some disciples into Jerusalem to find a place for them to have what would be their last Passover meal together before his crucifixion. As the sun went down, they gathered in what's referred to as the upper room. And then Jesus did the strangest thing. He took off his rabbinical robe, put a towel around his waist, and washed the disciples' feet.

They were indignant because Jesus was acting like a servant and they wanted him to act like they imagined the Messiah should act.

> He came to Simon Peter, who said to him, "Lord, are you going to wash my feet?"

> Jesus replied, "You do not realize now what I am doing, but later you will understand."

> "No," said Peter, "you shall never wash my feet."
> Jesus answered, "Unless I wash you, you have no part with me." John 13:6–8

And then this:

> When he had finished washing their feet, he put on his
> clothes and returned to his place. "Do you understand
> what I have done for you?" he asked them. "You call
> me 'Teacher' and 'Lord,' and rightly so, for that is what
> I am. Now that I, your Lord and Teacher, have washed
> your feet, you also should wash one another's feet. I
> have set you an example that you should do as I have
> done for you. John 13:12–15

To us, this is a story about Jesus setting an example of servant leadership. To his disciples, it was upsetting to see their rabbi humbled to the point of washing their feet. This was not what they had signed on for.

Later they retired to the garden of Gethsemane to pray. In the middle of the night, while Jesus was isolated from the crowds that followed him, Judas made his move. The high priest and the temple guard arrested Jesus. The events that would lead to his crucifixion were set in motion.

Everything was working out exactly as God had planned, because God's hand cannot be forced, and God's will cannot be thwarted.

In the end, Judas' greatest regret—just like our greatest regrets—was associated with an attempt to hang on to something that turned out to be unimportant. Judas' greatest regret was his attempt to force God's hand.

When Judas, who had betrayed him, saw that Jesus was condemned, he was seized with remorse and returned the thirty pieces of silver to the chief priests and the elders. "I have sinned," he said, "for I have betrayed innocent blood."

"What is that to us?" they replied. "That's your responsibility."

So Judas threw the money into the temple and left. Then he went away and hanged himself. Matthew 27:3–5

VIDEO NOTES

DISCUSSION QUESTIONS

1. Have you ever tried to bargain with God? What happened?

2. Talk about a time when you lost patience with God. What did you do? What happened as a result?

3. Do you agree that our greatest regrets are associated with trying to hang on to something that turned out to be unimportant? Why or why not?

4. The disciples were uncomfortable with Jesus serving them by washing their feet. They didn't like to see their rabbi humbled in that way. Does the idea that Jesus served you by dying for your sins make you uncomfortable? If so, why?

5. Can you think of a time when you refused to surrender to God because you wanted what you wanted? In what ways were you responsible for the outcome of that decision?

6. During last week's discussion, you talked about something you're currently trying to preserve that you need to surrender to God. Do you think the value of whatever it is you're trying to preserve may diminish over time? What would it look like to surrender it to God and let him take responsibility for the outcomes?

THINK ABOUT IT

When we decide something is more important than a relationship with our heavenly Father, whatever that thing is immediately begins to lose its appeal. When we barter or bargain with God, we are responsible for the outcome. That was the case with Judas Iscariot and it's the case with us.

This should scare us: God will not get in the way of us having our way. He won't rob us of the responsibility associated with our decisions.

That shouldn't scare us because God is scary. It should give us pause because God values our freedom so much that he will not interfere with it even when we undermine our own success or happiness. When Judas couldn't get Jesus to do his bidding, God didn't stop Judas from doing what he wanted. In the end, Judas traded his relationship with Jesus for something that immediately began to devalue. And nothing Judas did thwarted God's will.

When we surrender, God takes responsibility for the outcome of the journey. When we finally decide that what we think we want isn't worth losing our integrity or violating our conscience, then God takes charge of our lives. And he's a lot better at it than we are.

BEFORE THE NEXT SESSION

To prepare for your next session, read the Overview for Session Three. You can also look through the Discussion Questions if you want to.

During the week, spend some time each day reading:

- Matthew 27
- Luke 23

[THE GOD WHO CAN BE TRUSTED]

Let's talk about the relationship between life and God. For many of us, life and God get confused. They appear to be one and the same. When life is good, God is good. When life is not good, God is not good. If life gets really tough and we experience extraordinary disappointment, it's easy to assume there is no God at all.

Disappointment with life becomes disappointment with God.

It's a tough pill to swallow when your dreams don't come true and the people around you tell you to just pray and trust God. After a while, you begin to equate your life experience with God. You decide God is not good, God is not personal, God is not active, or perhaps there is no God at all.

But what makes this so complicated is if you were taught that God is behind everything, then it's easy to confuse your life experiences with

God. It becomes virtually impossible to prevent your frustrations with life from becoming frustrations with God.

That's why it's important to understand that our circumstances are not a measure of how much God loves us or whether he's pleased with us.

OVERVIEW

This session we're going to talk about a character whose life spun out of control by the time his path crossed with Jesus'. We don't know how old he was. We don't know his name. But we do know he ended up in a Roman jail cell.

He was condemned to death because he was so violent and unpredictable, he couldn't even be trusted as a slave. He couldn't even be trusted to row a Roman galley. His only value was to illustrate the futility of defying Rome. They condemned him to death by crucifixion as a warning to others who might consider breaking Rome's laws.

This man had seen crucifixions. He'd seen the aftermath of crucifixions. He knew exactly what he was in for. He would fight and curse and scream. He would be defiant, but death would eventually take him. His body would be taken from the cross, put on a wagon, carted to the south side of Jerusalem into the valley of Gehenna, and left in the city dump because no one would be given permission to claim it.

But this man decided he would die the way he lived: defiantly. And on the morning they dragged him out of that jail cell, he discovered two other people would be crucified that same day. One was another criminal, like himself. The other was Jesus, the Jewish rabbi from Nazareth.

It's important to understand that crucifixion was a terrible way to die. It was hours and hours of pain, terror, and humiliation. In some instances, it took two or three days for a crucified person to die.

As all of this misery was taking place, the two criminals heard Jesus say about the people gathered to watch these executions, "Father, forgive them, for they do not know what they are doing" (Luke 23:34). While the crowd mocked him and the Roman soldiers split up everything he owned and gambled to see who could win all of it back, Jesus prayed for them. People had gathered from all over town because everyone came to see a crucifixion.

There's something about tragedy and pain that is embarrassingly fascinating. We can't look away.

But it wasn't just the common people of Jerusalem who had come to see Jesus die. The rulers—the very people that had Jesus arrested and crucified—were there. And these rulers sneered at him, "He saved others; let him save himself if he is God's Messiah, the Chosen One" (Luke 23:35). This was the group of people that had the most to lose from Jesus' success. From now on, they were in charge and this was their moment to take revenge.

The soldiers joined in as well. In Hollywood movie crucifixions, the crosses rise high from the ground and everyone looks up at the people being crucified. That's not how the Romans did it. They crucified people about six inches off the ground because the point of crucifixion was humiliation. These Roman soldiers were able to walk right up to Jesus, almost face to face. They were able to scream in his face and spit on him. They taunted Jesus: "If you are the king of the Jews, save yourself" (Luke 23:37).

The two criminals joined in as well. Now, here's an interesting detail: Luke wrote in his Gospel that one of the criminals hurled insults at Jesus (Luke 23:39). Remember, Luke was a Greek doctor who became a Christian years after the resurrection and wrote his

Gospel by interviewing eyewitnesses. But when Matthew, who was one of the 12 disciples and an eyewitness to these events, wrote his Gospel, he said *both* criminals turned their anger away from the crowd and toward Jesus (Matthew 27:44).

Take a moment and imagine this: Everyone in the crowd—the rulers, the soldiers, even the two criminals being crucified on either side of him—are mocking and insulting Jesus. Some of them are spitting on him. There was a reason Jesus had stirred this level of rage. Luke captures it in his Gospel:

> One of the criminals who hung there hurled insults at
> him: "Aren't you the Messiah? Save yourself and us!"
> Luke 23:39

Wasn't Jesus supposed to be able to do something about this? If he was the Messiah, couldn't he save himself and the criminals? And then suddenly in the middle of all of that chaos and pain, the criminal stops shouting insults because something so unimaginable happens that he recognizes in an instant there's something different about this crucified rabbi:

> Jesus said, "Father, forgive them, for they do not know
> what they are doing." Luke 23:34

And it dawns on the criminal that Jesus is a righteous man, sent from God. He confronts the other criminal:

> "Don't you fear God," he said, "since you are under the same sentence? We are punished justly, for we are getting what our deeds deserve. But this man has done nothing wrong." Luke 23:39–41

Here was a man suffering unjustly, but who still believed that God could be called Father. Jesus was not drawing conclusions about God based on the way life and others were treating him. Suddenly, for the criminal, there was a new category. He was beginning to see Jesus in a way that no one in the crowd was seeing him.

In the final moments of his life, Jesus had a conversation with a criminal—not a righteous man. This was possibly one of the least righteous men in Jerusalem. That criminal had realized that if an innocent man suffering like a guilty man could maintain faith in God, then a guilty man who deserved his punishment ought to be able to do the same. And in that moment, the criminal realized that Jesus really was the Messiah.

> Then he said, "Jesus, remember me when you come into your kingdom."

Jesus answered him, "Truly I tell you, today you will be with me in paradise." Luke 23:42–43

The criminal asked Jesus to remember him when he came into his kingdom, not *because* of anything the criminal had done but *in spite* of everything he'd done. If Jesus could maintain faith in a good and just God in the midst of those terrible circumstances, perhaps there was a good and just God after all.

Jesus' answer that the criminal would be with him in paradise is important for us to hear. Jesus didn't say that because the criminal had rededicated his life. Rededicating your life while you're hanging from a cross is meaningless. There is no turning over a new leaf when you're going to spend the remaining few hours of your life nailed to a tree. All the criminal could offer was a desperate plea for grace and mercy.

Jesus was merciful because his thoughts about us are not reflected in what's happening to us. His love for us is not reflected in our circumstances. What if it's true that God is not your personal experience? What if God loves you even when life has left you broken?

VIDEO NOTES

_____

_____

_____

_____

_____

_____

_____

_____

_____

_____

_____

_____

_____

_____

_____

_____

_____

_____

_____

DISCUSSION QUESTIONS

1. Did you grow up in a faith tradition that observed Lent? If so, what was your experience? Does observing Lent currently play a role in your spiritual experience of Easter? If not, could it?

2. In general, do you tend to think of God as being pleased with you or disappointed in you? What has shaped those assumptions about God's view of you?

3. Have you ever felt disappointed with God because you were in a disappointing season of life? If so, what happened?

4. Read Luke 23:42-43 aloud together. What do you think about Jesus accepting the criminal even though he was beyond the point of being able to change his life? Does it seem fair to you? What implications might it have in your own life?

5. What if it's true that God is not your personal experience? What if God loves you even when life has left you broken? How might that change the way you live out your faith?

6. In what ways do you still try to earn God's love? What are some practical things you can do to accept the grace he freely offers and to obey him, not in order to earn his love, but because he already loves you?

THINK ABOUT IT

In the temple in Jerusalem, a heavy curtain separated the Holy of Holies (the small room where God's presence was said to dwell) from the rest of the temple. Only certain priests could go behind that curtain and only at specific times for specific reasons. The Holy of Holies was a serious place because entering into God's presence was serious business.

Matthew's Gospel records an extraordinary event that happened when Jesus died on the cross:

> At that moment the curtain of the temple was torn in two from top to bottom. The earth shook, the rocks split and the tombs broke open ... Matthew 27:51–52

In that moment, everything that separated human beings from God was torn away through the death of Jesus. So, here's the question: Have you allowed your circumstances to cause you to confuse life with God? *Have you drawn conclusions about God based on what has happened to you?* It's natural to do so. It may even be unavoidable. But it's not true.

Jesus' message to you from the cross is this: God—your heavenly Father—is not what you have experienced. You can trust him despite your experiences.

God is not your life.

God sent Jesus to bring you life.

BEFORE THE NEXT SESSION

To prepare for your next session, read the Overview for Session Four. You can also look through the Discussion Questions if you want to.

During the week, spend some time each day reading:

- Luke 24
- John 20
- 1 Peter 1

SESSION FOUR

[THE FOUNDATION OF OUR FAITH]

No one expected Jesus to rise from the dead—not even his closest followers. We wouldn't have expected it either. We would've expected Jesus to do exactly what dead people do—they stay dead.

This is why in the Gospel accounts, no one is waiting outside of Jesus' tomb counting down toward the big moment. No one was outside the tomb because they expected Jesus to stay dead. They did exactly what anyone would do who expected Jesus to stay dead.

The text tells us that when the Sabbath was over and Jesus' followers were free to do work, Mary Magdalene and a group of women purchased spices to re-embalm Jesus' body. The reason they had to purchase them after the Sabbath was because the events of the crucifixion had unfolded so quickly, they hadn't had time to purchase them.

Jesus was arrested Thursday night and by Friday evening, he was dead and buried. It all happened so quickly, there was no way for them to catch up emotionally. All they knew—all they assumed—was that the movement Jesus had started died with him.

And so Mary Magdalene and the other women did the only thing they knew to do: purchase the spices to re-embalm Jesus' body so they could finish the burial, finish the movement, and begin to figure out what was next in their lives.

OVERVIEW

Jesus' closest followers believed he was a teacher and a miracle worker from God. They had hoped he was the Messiah. But they were wrong. God would not allow his Messiah to be crucified. And they had watched Jesus die. They had followed Nicodemus and Joseph of Arimathea, who probably paid Pontius Pilate to get Jesus' body. They watched these two men hurriedly embalm Jesus' body and place it in a fresh tomb.

After Passover, they decided they'd try to get inside the tomb and take the time they didn't have earlier to properly prepare Jesus' body and, more important, to say their final goodbyes. This would be closure. It would be their way of closing the book on this chapter of their lives.

But Luke's Gospel tells us what happened next:

> They found the stone rolled away from the tomb, but when they entered, they did not find the body of the Lord Jesus. Luke 24:2–3

When Jesus' closest followers peered into the empty tomb, not a single one of them assumed a resurrection. When Mary and the group of women peered into that empty tomb, they assumed exactly what we would assume: Someone had stolen the body.

John's Gospel says:

> So she came running to Simon Peter and the other disciple, the one Jesus loved, and said, "They have taken the Lord out of the tomb, and we don't know where they have put him!" John 20:2

Luke says that the disciples were so skeptical because of how frantic and emotional the women were. They didn't believe them. If you acknowledge that Jesus was a historical person and you agree he taught some good things, but you think the resurrection part of the story is nonsense, you're in good company. Jesus' best friends felt the same way on the morning they discovered his body was gone. None of them assumed resurrection. Again, they assumed what everyone would: that Jesus would stay dead. But Peter and John were being told that Jesus' body had been taken from the tomb. They couldn't just sit there, so they headed for the tomb:

> Both were running, but the other disciple outran Peter and reached the tomb first. He bent over and looked in at the strips of linen lying there but did not go in. Then Simon Peter came along behind him and went straight into the tomb. He saw the strips of linen lying there, as well as the cloth that had been wrapped around Jesus' head. The cloth was still lying in its place, separate from the linen. Finally the other disciple, who had reached the tomb first, also went inside. He saw and believed. (They still did not understand from Scripture that Jesus had to rise from the dead.) Then the disciples went back to where they were staying. John 20:4–10

Notice how they documented their own disbelief. These were not superstitious people. These were men and women who had given up hope. There was no dream to keep alive. There was no movement to keep moving.

They were hiding from the religious leaders in Jerusalem the evening after they discovered the empty tomb when Jesus paid them a visit. They were startled. They were frightened.

> He said to them, "Why are you troubled, and why do doubts rise in your minds? Look at my hands and my feet. It is I myself! Touch me and see; a ghost does not have flesh and bones, as you see I have."
>
> When he had said this, he showed them his hands and feet. Luke 24:38–40

And then he looked them in the eye and said something so extraordinarily important it would not only change their lives but human history.

> He said to them, "This is what I told you while I was still with you: Everything must be fulfilled that is written about me in the Law of Moses, the Prophets and the Psalms."
>
> Then he opened their minds so they could understand the Scriptures. He told them, "This is what is written: The Messiah will suffer and rise from the dead on the

third day, and repentance for the forgiveness of sins
will be preached in his name to all nations, beginning
at Jerusalem. You are witnesses of these things. I am
going to send you what my Father has promised; but
stay in the city until you have been clothed with power
from on high." Luke 24:44–49

The disciples were witnesses to the event that changed the world.
They were witnesses to the event that launched the church. They
were witnesses to the resurrection of Jesus.

The church didn't create the Bible. The church didn't create the
story of Jesus. The resurrection of Jesus launched the church
and created our faith. Before the resurrection, there were no
Christians. After Jesus was crucified, there were no believers. His
followers gave up hope. Hope didn't return until they saw Jesus
alive with their own eyes.

The reason we believe Jesus rose from the dead isn't because
the Bible tells us so. It's because of the testimony of Jesus'
closest followers. We believe Jesus rose from the dead because
skeptical eyewitnesses wrote down the extraordinary event they
had watched.

Peter, who peered dumbfounded into the empty tomb, later dictated these words:

> Praise be to the God and Father of our Lord Jesus Christ! In his great mercy he has given us new birth into a living hope through the resurrection of Jesus Christ from the dead . . . 1 Peter 1:3

If you could ask Peter what the foundation of his faith was, he wouldn't say Jesus' teachings. He would say the resurrection. By dying on the cross for our sin, Jesus paved the way for us to have a relationship with God—a relationship described as that between a perfect father and a child.

VIDEO NOTES

_____

_____

_____

_____

_____

_____

_____

_____

_____

_____

_____

_____

_____

_____

_____

_____

_____

_____

_____

_____

DISCUSSION QUESTIONS

1. What are you looking forward to during this Easter season? Why?

2. On a scale of 1 to 10, how much do you struggle with the question of why a good God would allow bad things to happen to good people? Has Jesus' resurrection changed your perspective on that question at all? Why or why not?

3. In the video teaching, Andy said, "It wasn't the teachings of Jesus that convinced Peter and the others. It was the resurrection of Jesus that completely reframed their lives." Do you agree? Why or why not?

4. Is the implausibility of the resurrection a stumbling block in your faith or has it been in the past? If so, does it help to know Jesus' own disciples weren't expecting him to rise from the dead?

5. What can you do this Easter to remind yourself that God intervened in human history in order to rescue *you*?

6. God loves you so much, he sent his only Son to die in order to set you free from sin and to adopt you as a child into his family. How does that change your perspective on faith? How does it change your perspective on life?

THINK ABOUT IT

Peter's and the other disciples' faith wasn't tethered to an imaginary God who doesn't allow bad things to happen to good people. That wasn't their God. If you've lost faith in God because of the evil and suffering in the world, or if you've lost faith in God because of your pain and suffering, we want to invite you to reconsider.

The men and women who brought us the story of Jesus saw pain and suffering most of us couldn't imagine, yet they believed. They saw the worst thing imaginable happen to the best person they had ever known, yet they believed because their faith was not in an imaginary god that never allowed bad things to happen to good people. Their faith was in the God introduced to them by Jesus—the God who invites you to address him as heavenly Father.

It wasn't the teachings of Jesus that convinced Peter and the others. It was the resurrection of Jesus that completely reframed their lives.

The invitation of Easter is to allow the resurrection of Jesus to reframe your life as well.

When Peter was confronted by the horror and violence of the crucifixion, he ran for his life. After the resurrection, that same man walked toward danger in order to give his life away.

Near the end of his life, Peter wrote the following words. He had no way of knowing that they would survive across centuries and be as relevant to our lives as they were to the first-century Christians he originally wrote them for:

> For you know that it was not with perishable things such as silver or gold that you were redeemed from the empty way of life handed down to you from your ancestors, but with the precious blood of Christ, a lamb without blemish or defect. He was chosen before the creation of the world, but was revealed in these last times for your sake. Through him you believe in God, who raised him from the dead and glorified him, and so your faith and hope are in God. 1 Peter 1:18–21

BEFORE EASTER

We hope you enjoyed this study and that you connected more with your group and had some great conversations. During the time you have between the end of this study and Easter Sunday, try to slow down your pace. Use this time to connect in meaningful ways with your heavenly Father.

We recommend you spend some time reading Matthew 27–28, Mark 15–16, Luke 23–24, and John 19–20. If you have time, read each chapter a few times over the course of a week. Each time you read a chapter, pause to think about what details stood out to you (maybe for the first time).

Spend some time praying as well. Most of us spend a lot of our prayer time asking God for things we need or want. Instead, focus on thanking him for providing what you *really* needed: a Savior.

[LEADER'S GUIDE]

LEADING THE DISCUSSION

You probably have a mental picture of what it will look like to lead— what you'll say and how group members will respond. Before you get too far into planning, there are some things you should know about leading a small-group discussion.

CULTIVATE DISCUSSION

It's easy to assume that a group meeting lives or dies on the quality of your ideas. That's not true. It's the ideas of everyone in the group that make a small-group meeting successful. Your role is to create an environment in which people feel safe to share their thoughts. That's how relationships will grow and thrive among your group members.

Here's a basic truth about spiritual growth within the context of community: the study materials aren't as important as the relationships through which those materials take practical shape in the lives of the group members. The more meaningful the relationships, the more meaningful the study. The best materials in the world won't change lives in a sterile environment.

POINT TO THE MATERIAL

Good hosts and hostesses create environments where people can connect relationally. They know when to help guests connect and when to stay out of the way when those connections are happening organically. As a small-group leader, sometimes you'll simply read a discussion question and invite everyone to respond. The conversation will take care of itself. At other times, you may need to encourage group members to share their ideas. Remember, some of the best insights will come from the people in your group. Go with the flow but be ready to nudge the conversation in the right direction when necessary.

DEPART FROM THE MATERIAL

We've carefully designed this study for your small group. We've written the materials and designed the questions to elicit the kinds of conversations we think will be most helpful to your group members. That doesn't mean you should stick rigidly to the materials. Knowing when to depart from them is more art than science, and no one knows more about your group than you do.

The stories, questions, and exercises are here to provide a framework for exploration. But different groups have different chemistries and different motivations. Sometimes the best way to start a small-group discussion is to ask, "Does anyone have a personal insight you'd like to share from this week's material?" Then sit back and listen.

STAY ON TRACK

This is the flip side to the previous point. There's an art to facilitating an engaging conversation. While you want to leave space for group members to think through the discussion, you also need to keep your objectives in mind. Make sure the discussion is contributing to the bottom line for the week. Don't let it veer off into tangents. Interject politely in order to refocus the group.

PRAY

This is the most important thing you can do as a leader. The best leaders get out of God's way and let him communicate through them. Remember: books don't teach God's Word; neither do sermons or discussion groups. God speaks into the hearts of men and women. Prayer is a vital part of communicating with him. Pray for your group members. Pray for your own leadership. Pray that God is not only present at your group meetings but is directing them.

SESSION ONE
THE HIGH COST OF FOLLOWING CHRIST

BIG IDEA

When you decide to follow Jesus, it will cost you something. But whatever you've replaced God with is less than God.

REFLECT

As you prepare to lead each session, we'll provide some relevant Bible passages to read and some guidance for reflecting on those passages. This is designed in part to give you some time to think about the Scriptures you'll be discussing with your group. More important, we hope daily reading will help you connect with your heavenly Father during this Easter season.

DAY 1
Read Matthew 23:1–12.

In this passage, Jesus singles out the teachers of the law, but we're all guilty of hypocrisy sometimes. Reflect on the areas of your own life in which your actions don't align with your beliefs. Think about what it would look like if you could more consistently behave based on what you believe.

DAY 2

Read Matthew 23:13–39.

What stood out to you most in this passage? Were there verses that hit particularly close to home? If so, pray about those things. Be honest with God and ask him for help.

DAY 3

Read John 12:1–11.

What stands out about Judas Iscariot's behavior? What is the relationship between self-righteousness and hypocrisy? Have you seen modern-day examples of this among Christians?

DAY 4

Read John 11:38–57.

Think about the people in this story—what they were feeling and thinking. Do you find this story moving? Why or why not?

DAY 5

Read Mark 12:13–17.

This passage records one of many incidents in which religious leaders tried to trap Jesus with a clever question. What do you find remarkable about Jesus' answer? If the denarius belonged to Caesar because it bore his image, what belongs to God? (Hint: see Genesis 1:27.)

PRAY

This week, spend some time praying the following prayer (you don't have to pray it verbatim; you can use your own words):

Father in Heaven,

I really do want you in the center of my life. I know your will is better for me than my desires. But I also struggle with wanting to be in control of my own life. I sometimes want to preserve what I have instead of trusting you. Help me accept your love. Help me accept your will for my life.

Amen.

DISCUSSION QUESTIONS

Use these notes to help you guide the group discussion:

1. What do you hope to experience this Easter season? Do you usually observe Easter as a spiritual season, celebrate it as a holiday, or both?

This is a simple icebreaker question, but listen to how group members answer. If people express a desire to connect with God in new and meaningful ways during the Easter season, make it a point to encourage one another. You might even choose to do an Easter devotion together.

2. During the message, Andy said, "When you decide to follow Jesus, it will cost you something." If you are a Jesus follower, what is something following has cost you?

This may be a challenging question for some group members. Be ready with your own example. It will encourage others to open up.

3. What's intimidating about the idea that God's will can't be thwarted? What's comforting?

This question is about exploring the tension we feel about God's sovereignty. On the one hand, it's comforting to know that he is in charge. On the other hand, it can be frustrating when we don't get what we want. Talking about that tension may normalize it for some group members.

4. Read John 11:38–44 aloud as a group. What do verses 41 and 42 indicate about Jesus' intent in raising Lazarus from the dead?

An important aspect of the Lazarus story is Jesus' intent to accelerate his ministry on earth. He knew that raising a man from the dead would increase his conflict with Jewish religious leaders. If your group members aren't quite sure how to answer the question, a good follow-up may be: "Why is it important that Jesus doesn't avoid doing things he knows will antagonize the religious authorities?"

Give your group members space to think before speaking. Try to get comfortable with uncomfortable silences. Resist offering your response first, if possible.

5. Read John 11:45–50 aloud as a group. How do verses 49 and 50 demonstrate the human capacity for justifying wrongdoing? Talk

about a time when you convinced yourself that something morally or ethically wrong was the right thing to do. What happened?

This is a challenging question. Have your own example ready in order to encourage your group members to share theirs.

6. What are you currently trying to preserve that you need to surrender to God? What is one thing you can do this week to begin to let go? How can this group support you?

The more specific your group members are, the more helpful this question will be. If they can identify a concrete, achievable action step, it will increase the odds they will follow through. It will also be more realistic for the group to offer encouragement and accountability. Again, be ready with your own example—including a clear idea of how you want the group's support. This will help your group members follow your lead.

Note: *Jot down some notes on how your group members answer this question. You'll revisit their answers in the next session.*

[SESSION TWO
THE RISK OF SURRENDERING TO GOD]

BIG IDEA

When we bargain with God, we are responsible for the outcome. When we surrender, God takes responsibility for the outcome of the journey.

REFLECT

As you prepare to lead each session, we'll provide some relevant Bible passages to read and some guidance for reflecting on those passages. This is designed in part to give you some time to think about the Scriptures you'll be discussing with your group. More important, we hope daily reading will help you connect with your heavenly Father during this Easter season.

DAY 1

Read Matthew 19:16–30.

Can you relate at all to the rich young ruler? Does the thought of sacrificing creature comforts in order to follow Jesus disturb you? If so, what can you do to remind yourself that what Jesus offers you is infinitely more valuable than what he requires of you?

DAY 2

Read John 12:1–11.

What details in this passage jump out at you? If you've read the passage before, did you notice anything new? What is your response to Jesus' statement: "You will always have the poor among you, but you will not always have me"?

DAY 3

Read Matthew 26:14–16.

Reread the passage a few times, trying to pick up on more details each time you read it. What emotions does the passage stir in you? Why do you think it stirs those emotions?

DAY 4

Read John 13:1–17.

This is one of the most famous stories in the New Testament. As you read it, are any details new to you? How do you think you would have responded if you'd been in that room and Jesus knelt before you to wash your feet? Why do you think you would respond that way?

DAY 5

Read Matthew 27:1–10.

Judas Iscariot is often thought of as a "bad guy," but in this passage we see him full of regret and despair. He had betrayed a friend and couldn't live with it any longer. How does this passage change your perspective on Judas? Does it make it easier to relate to him?

PRAY

This week, spend some time praying the following prayer (you don't have to do it verbatim; you can use your own words):

> Dear God,
>
> It scares me to think I'm like Judas Iscariot. I want to surrender everything to you, but that's hard for me to do. I recognize that I'm better off when you're responsible for outcomes. But I still want what I want. Father, soften my heart and loosen my grip on my life so I can learn to give you more and more control. I know you're trustworthy.
>
> Amen.

DISCUSSION QUESTIONS

Use these notes to help you guide the group discussion:

1. Have you ever tried to bargain with God? What happened?

This question can function as an icebreaker, but it also has the potential to draw your group into a deep discussion. It depends on how vulnerable group members choose to be. Don't force the issue. If the conversation stays light, that's okay. If you want it to go a little deeper, be prepared to share an example from your own life.

2. Talk about a time when you lost patience with God. What did you do? What happened as a result?

Group members may respond to this question with different levels of openness and vulnerability. That's okay. The important thing is to understand that we've all experienced negative emotions about God. It's normal, even for those who follow him.

If a group member is struggling with guilt over a past experience, remind them that God is big enough to handle their emotions. King David often expressed negative emotions in the Psalms. God didn't reject or abandon him.

3. Do you agree that our greatest regrets are associated with trying to hang on to something that turned out to be unimportant? Why or why not?

Give group members the space to disagree. It's okay to express your opinion on the matter, but don't try to correct them or convince them to change their minds. Listen to what others have to say. Thank them for their opinions.

4. The disciples were uncomfortable with Jesus serving them by washing their feet. They didn't like to see their rabbi humbled in that way. Does the idea that Jesus served you by dying for your sins make you uncomfortable? If so, why?

It's normal for people to feel uncomfortable with their need for Jesus' sacrifice. We want to earn grace. It feels almost unnatural that God would give it to us as a gift even though we don't deserve it. Be forthright with your own opinion. Listen to the opinions of others. Don't try to bring the entire group to an agreement on the matter.

5. Can you think of a time when you refused to surrender to God because you wanted what you wanted? In what ways were you responsible for the outcome of that decision?

This may be an uncomfortable question for some group members to answer. It may be associated with the most challenging seasons in their lives. Don't push people to share, but try to create an environment where they feel safe to do so. The best way to accomplish that is to be open with your own story.

6. During last week's discussion, you talked about something you're currently trying to preserve that you need to surrender to God. Do you think the value of whatever it is you're trying to preserve may diminish over time? What would it look like to surrender it to God and let him take responsibility for the outcomes?

Remember how you took notes on group members' answers to Question 6 last session? Now is the time to use those notes. Ask people if they followed through on the action steps they identified and how it went. If someone didn't follow through, tell them it's okay. There's no need to feel guilty. But let them know you'd love for them to apply what you're discussing in this study. It will help them grow in their relationship with God.

[SESSION THREE
THE GOD WHO CAN BE TRUSTED]

BIG IDEA

Your heavenly Father is not what you have experienced. You can trust him despite your experiences.

REFLECT

As you prepare to lead each session, we'll provide some relevant Bible passages to read and some guidance for reflecting on those passages. This is designed in part to give you some time to think about the Scriptures you'll be discussing with your group. More important, we hope daily reading will help you connect with your heavenly Father during this Easter season.

Each day this week, you'll read one of the accounts of Jesus' arrest, trial, and crucifixion in each of the Gospels. As you read a particular account, reflect on its details. What does it emphasize? What details does it include that other Gospels don't? What details does it omit that other Gospels include? Why do you think each author chose the details he did? What ideas was he trying to get across?

On Day 5, revisit Matthew 27 and Luke 23. These are the accounts you'll focus on during your group discussion.

DAY 1

Reread Matthew 27.

DAY 2

Read Mark 15.

DAY 3

Read Luke 23.

DAY 4

Read John 19.

DAY 5

Read Matthew 27 and Luke 23.

PRAY

This week, spend some time praying the following prayer (you don't have to pray it verbatim; you can use your own words):

Dear Lord,

I confess that too often I mistake the circumstances of my life with who you are. Something in me wants to believe that my relationship with you entitles me to a pain-free existence. I know that's not true. I know you are trustworthy. I know you are full of grace and mercy and truth. I know you love me.

Help me to live in your truth ... through all circumstances, whatever they are.

Amen.

DISCUSSION QUESTIONS

1. Did you grow up in a faith tradition that observed Lent? If so, what was your experience? Does observing Lent currently play a role in your spiritual experience of Easter? If not, could it?

You don't need to spend more than a few minutes on this icebreaker, but it can be helpful for group members to hear about one another's experiences with spiritual practices. They may inspire one another to try new approaches for connecting with God.

2. In general, do you tend to think of God as being pleased with you or disappointed in you? What has shaped those assumptions about God's view of you?

This is a big question. Sometimes people know the theological truth that God is loving and merciful, but because of past experiences it's still hard for them to accept that truth in their own lives. Depending on what they were taught about God when they were young, it can be difficult to let go of the idea that God is disappointed in them.

Listen to what your group members have to say. Offer encouragement and reassurance, if necessary.

3. Have you ever felt disappointed with God because you were in a disappointing season of life? If so, what happened?

The best discussion around this question will happen if people feel safe to open up and be honest. Don't judge people's answers. Don't correct them with theology or quote Bible verses at them. Listen. Thank them for sharing. Let them know that times of disappointment with God are a normal part of everyone's faith. Disappointment may not be rational, but being open with God about how we feel is essential to growing closer to him.

4. Read Luke 23:42–43 aloud together. What do you think about Jesus accepting the criminal even though he was beyond the point of being able to change his life? Does it seem fair to you? What implications might it have in your own life?

These verses are simple. They can also be hard to swallow. Because they are a perfect picture of grace, they seem unfair to many people. They are unfair. The criminal receives what he doesn't deserve because that is the nature of grace. We want to believe that we're different than the criminal, that we deserve God's favor. But we're not and we don't.

5. What if it's true that God is not your personal experience? What if God loves you even when life has left you broken? How might that change the way you live out your faith?

This question encourages your group members to imagine a different spiritual reality than what they may currently be experiencing. The point is not to come to a "right" answer. It's to imagine new possibilities. Imagining those possibilities may inspire some of your group members to pursue them.

6. In what ways do you still try to earn God's love? What are some practical things you can do to accept the grace he freely offers and to obey him, not in order to earn his love, but because he already loves you?

The more specific your group members can be in answering this question, the more successful they'll be in applying what they've learned. To help them, be ready to offer your own personal application. Be as specific as you can, because they'll probably only be as specific as you are.

[# SESSION FOUR
THE FOUNDATION OF OUR FAITH]

BIG IDEA

The church didn't create the story of Jesus. The resurrection of Jesus launched the church and created our faith.

REFLECT

DAY 1

Read Luke 24:1–12.

DAY 2

Read Luke 24:36–49.

As you read Luke's account of the resurrection on Days 1 and 2, just absorb and reflect on the details. Read the chapters a few times, and try to notice new things as you do.

DAY 3

Read John 20:1–23.

As you read John's account of the resurrection again, absorb and reflect on the details. While Luke was a highly educated man who based his account on the eyewitness details he carefully gathered, John was an eyewitness. How do you think that influences the level of detail and intent each man brought to his account?

DAY 4

Read 1 Peter 1:3–12.

This is a dense passage. Plan to read it a few times. Don't worry if you have to read certain sentences multiple times in order to begin to understand them. This is deep stuff. What stands out to you about Peter's observations of faith and hope? What value do you think this passage might offer if you were to return to it during a season of life when you felt hopeless?

DAY 5

Read 1 Peter 1:13–25.

Like the part of this passage you read on Day 4, this writing is dense. You'll probably need to read it a few times to begin to absorb it. What does it tell you about "holy" behavior that is motivated by hope in the resurrection versus holiness motivated by a desire to earn God's favor? Why is that distinction important? What can you do to pursue a faith motivated by hope in your Savior?

PRAY

This week, spend some time praying the following prayer (you don't have to do it verbatim; you can use your own words):

Father in Heaven,

Help me fully embrace the truth of the resurrection so I can allow it to reframe my life. Help me abandon any faith I'm holding on to in an imaginary god that never allows bad things to happen to good people. And give me the strength to embrace you as you truly are: my loving Creator who invites me to address him as Father.

Amen.

DISCUSSION QUESTIONS

1. What are you looking forward to during this Easter season? Why?

This is an icebreaker. Give people time to respond, but don't spend more than a few minutes on this question.

2. On a scale of 1 to 10, how much do you struggle with the question of why a good God would allow bad things to happen to good people? Has Jesus' resurrection changed your perspective on that question at all? Why or why not?

If a group member gives themselves a high rating, that's okay. This is a question theologians continue to wrestle with. There are no easy answers to this one, so don't try to offer one. Theology rarely offers satisfying answers to questions rooted in personal pain.

The question of why God allows suffering is mysterious. But Jesus' death and resurrection give us something important to hold on to— the knowledge that even when we don't understand God's motives, we can know that he loves us enough to sacrifice his one and only Son for us.

3. In the video teaching, Andy said, "It wasn't the teachings of Jesus that convinced Peter and the others. It was the resurrection of Jesus that completely reframed their lives." Do you agree? Why or why not?

Give people the space to disagree. This is a good question to practice the 80/20 rule on: listen 80 percent of the time and speak 20 percent.

4. Is the implausibility of the resurrection a stumbling block in your faith or has it been in the past? If so, does it help to know Jesus' own disciples weren't expecting him to rise from the dead?

It should go without saying that expressing doubt in a small group can be intimidating. Your group members are more likely to open up if they trust they won't be judged for their honesty. Listen to what they have to say. Don't try to answer all of the doubts. If you've ever experienced these doubts yourself, now is a good time to open up about them. It will encourage group members to do the same.

5. What can you do this Easter to remind yourself that God intervened in human history in order to rescue you?

Ideally, group members will come up with specific, concrete things they can do to remind themselves of God's faithfulness. Having your own specific example may help group members think of and communicate their own.

6. God loves you so much, he sent his only Son to die in order to set you free from sin and to adopt you as a child into his family. How does that change your perspective on faith? How does it change your perspective on life?

The idea of grace—that God loves us and gave his Son up for us, even though we don't deserve it—is difficult to accept in our hearts even when we understand it in our minds. Give group members space to express doubts. Listen. Thank them for sharing. Share your own experiences. Avoid responding by correcting behavior or offering simple theological answers.

Are we too familiar with Christmas and Easter?

The stories of Christmas and Easter are so familiar that we rarely dig into the details.

But what if we did?

We might find that they stop sounding like far-fetched fairy tales. In fact, the improbable details of these stories might even start to sound like real life—maybe even your life.

Who Need Christmas Study Guide 9780310121077	DVD 9780310121121	Why Easter Matters Study Guide 9780310121091

Available now at your favorite bookstore, or streaming video on StudyGateway.com.

Once upon a time there existed a version of our faith worth the world found irresistible.

In this book and six-session study, Andy Stanley shows us how Jesus' arrival signaled that the Old Testament was fulfilled and its laws reduced to a single verb—love—to be applied to God, neighbor, and enemy. So, what is required if we want to follow Jesus' example and radically love the people around us? We almost always know the answer. The hard part is actually doing what love requires.

Rather than working harder to make Christianity more interesting, we need to recover what once made faith in Jesus irresistible to the world.

Book	Study Guide	DVD
9780310536970	9780310100492	9780310100515

Available now at your favorite bookstore,
or streaming video on StudyGateway.com.

What Makes You Happy?
It's Not What You'd Expect

Everybody wants to be happy. Everybody is on a happiness quest. For many, happiness is measured in moments. Experiences. It's elusive. Unsustainable. What about you? What makes you happy?

In this remarkable six-part study, Andy reveals what makes you happy. He explores the three things all happy people have in common and how these three things can be realities for you as well.

Study Guide
9780310084990

DVD
9780310085010

Available now at your favorite bookstore,
or streaming video on StudyGateway.com

What if you could find a new starting point for faith?

Everything has a starting point—your life, your relationships, your education, your career. Your faith has a starting point as well. But too often, that faith isn't strong enough to withstand the pressures of life. So what if you could find a new starting point for faith?

Welcome to *Starting Point*—an eight-session small group conversation about faith. Whether you're new to faith, curious about God, or coming back to church after some time away, it's a place where your opinions and beliefs are valued, and no question is off limits.

Study Guide
9780310819325

DVD
9780310817734

Available now at your favorite bookstore,
or streaming video on StudyGateway.com.

Grow an Unshakable Faith

Imagine how different your outlook on life would be if you had absolute confidence that God was with you. Imagine how differently you would respond to difficulties, temptations, and even good things if you knew with certainty that God was in all of it and was planning to leverage it for good. In other words, imagine what it would be like to have perfect faith.

In this six-part series, Andy Stanley builds a biblical case for five things God uses to grow BIG faith.

Study Guide
9780310324232

DVD
9780310324188

Available now at your favorite bookstore,
or streaming video on StudyGateway.com.

ZONDERVAN®